AF531220

Art Styles

Renaissance

by Julie Murray

Dash!
LEVELED READERS
An Imprint of Abdo Zoom • abdobooks.com

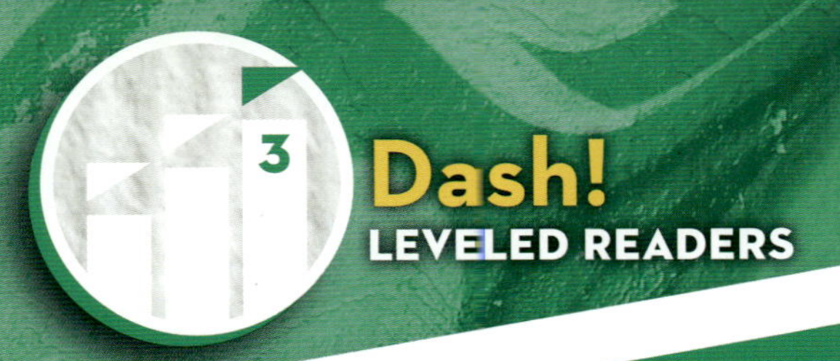

Level 1 – Beginning
Short and simple sentences with familiar words or patterns for children who are beginning to understand how letters and sounds go together.

Level 2 – Emerging
Longer words and sentences with more complex language patterns for readers who are practicing common words and letter sounds.

Level 3 – Transitional
More developed language and vocabulary for readers who are becoming more independent.

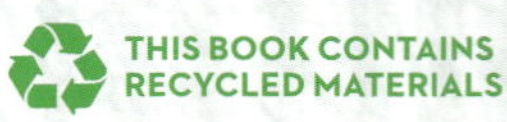

abdobooks.com

Published by Abdo Zoom, a division of ABDO, PO Box 398166, Minneapolis, Minnesota 55439.

Printed in the United States of America, North Mankato, Minnesota.
102023
012024

Photo Credits: Getty Images, Shutterstock, ©Torbjorn Toby Jorgensen p.10/ CC BY-SA 2.0
Production Contributors: Kenny Abdo, Jennie Forsberg, Grace Hansen, John Hansen
Design Contributors: Candice Keimig, Neil Klinepier

Library of Congress Control Number: 2023937949

Publisher's Cataloging in Publication Data

Names: Murray, Julie, author.
Title: Renaissance / by Julie Murray
Description: Minneapolis, Minnesota : Abdo Zoom, 2024 | Series: Art styles | Includes online resources and index.
Identifiers: ISBN 9781098283988 (lib. bdg.) | ISBN 9781098284701 (eBook) | ISBN 9781098285067 (Read-to-Me eBook)
Subjects: LCSH: Art, Renaissance--Juvenile literature. | Renaissance arts--Juvenile literature. | Art--15th century--Juvenile literature. Art--16th century--Juvenile literature.
Classification: DDC 709.024--dc23

Table of Contents

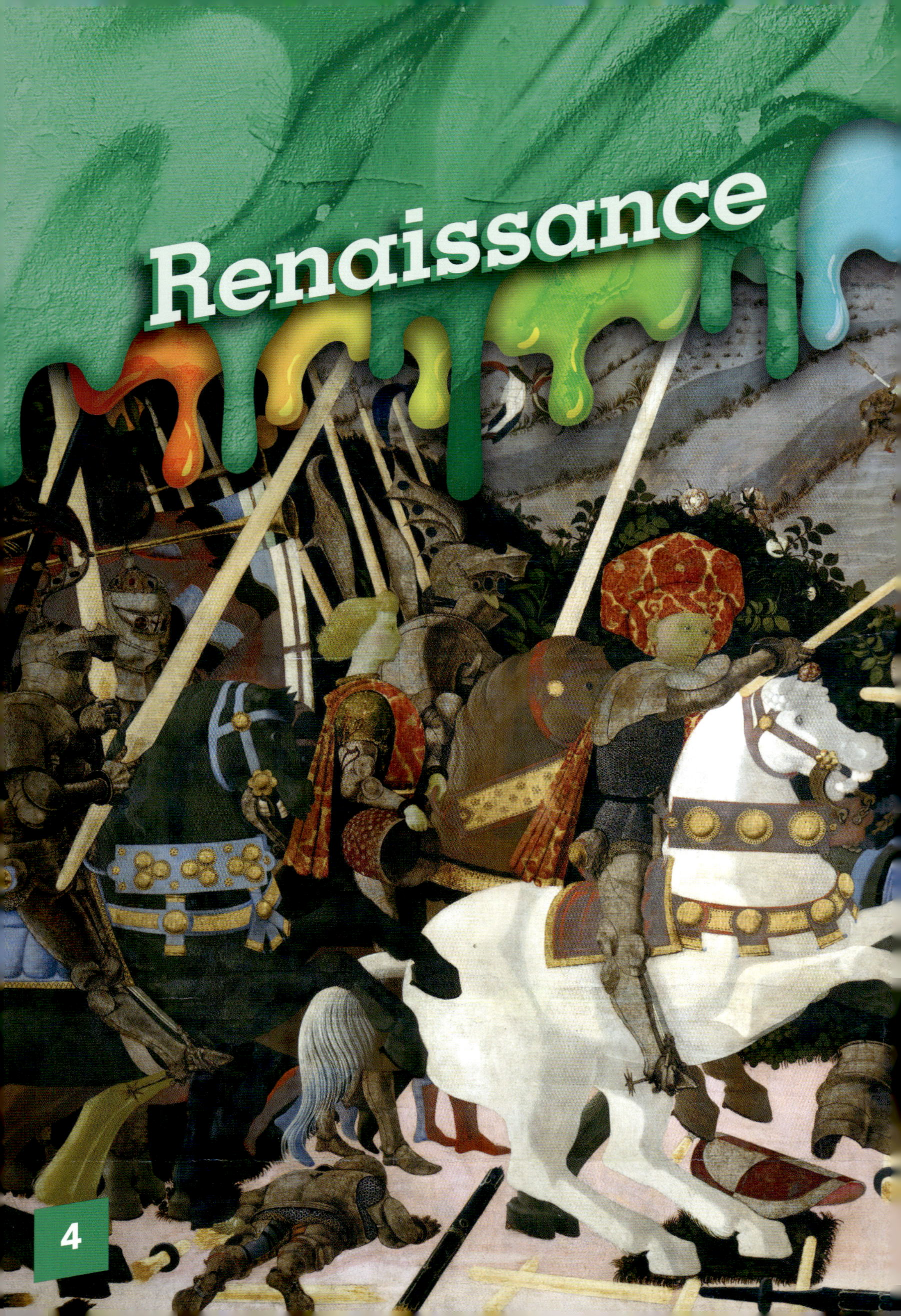

Renaissance

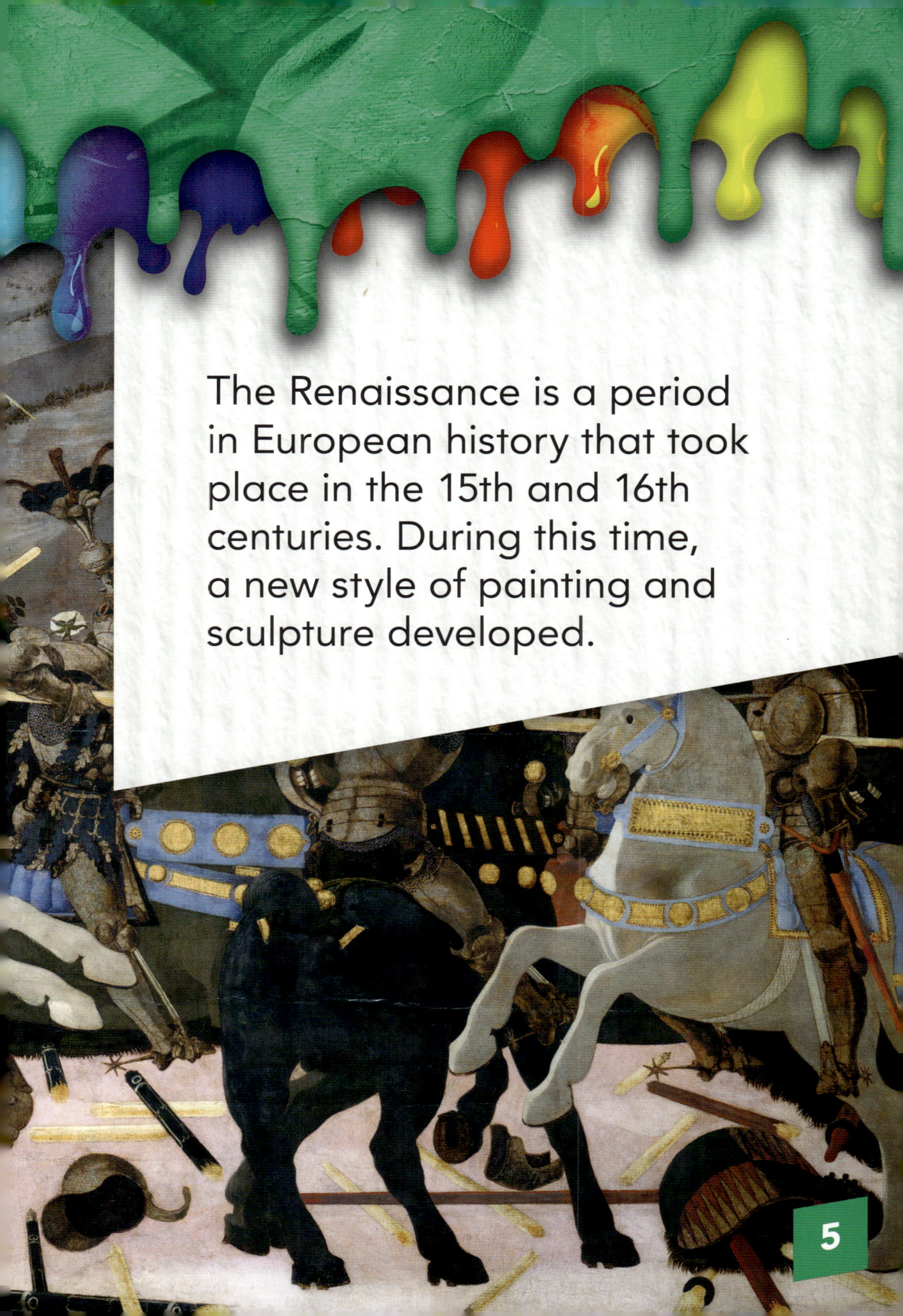

The Renaissance is a period in European history that took place in the 15th and 16th centuries. During this time, a new style of painting and sculpture developed.

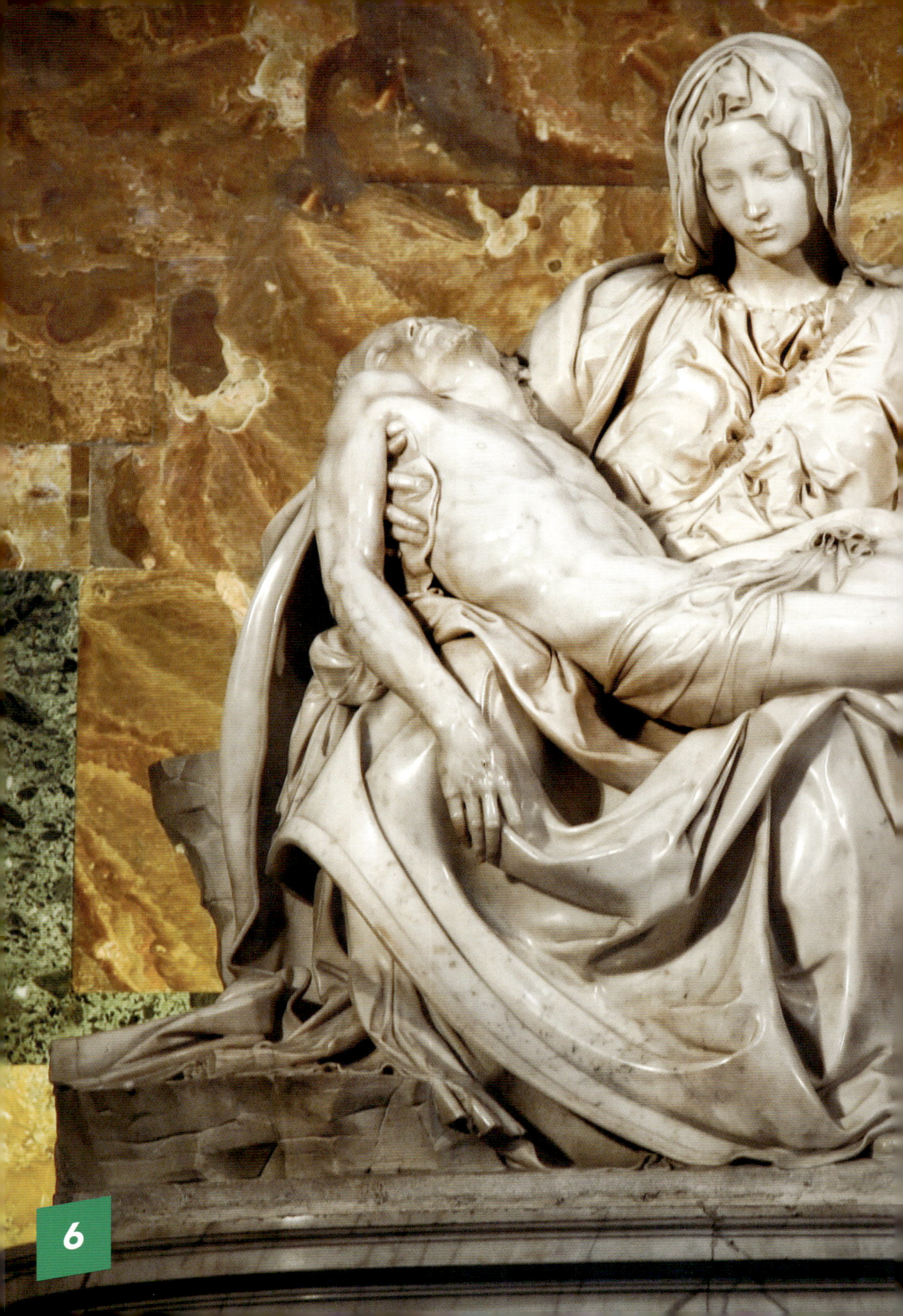

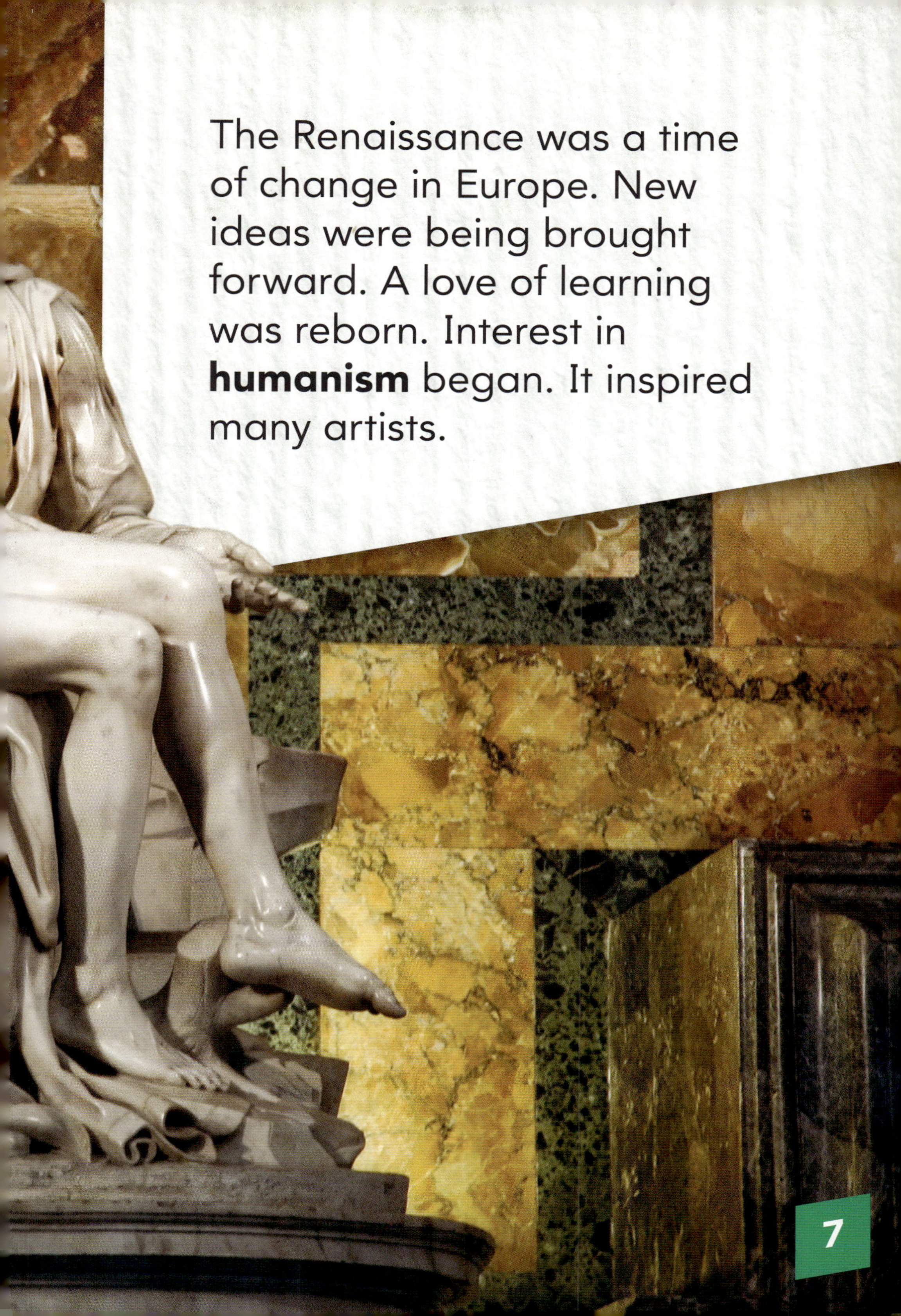

The Renaissance was a time of change in Europe. New ideas were being brought forward. A love of learning was reborn. Interest in **humanism** began. It inspired many artists.

The Medicis were a wealthy family who ruled Florence, Italy, in the 15th century. They loved art and helped fund the Renaissance.

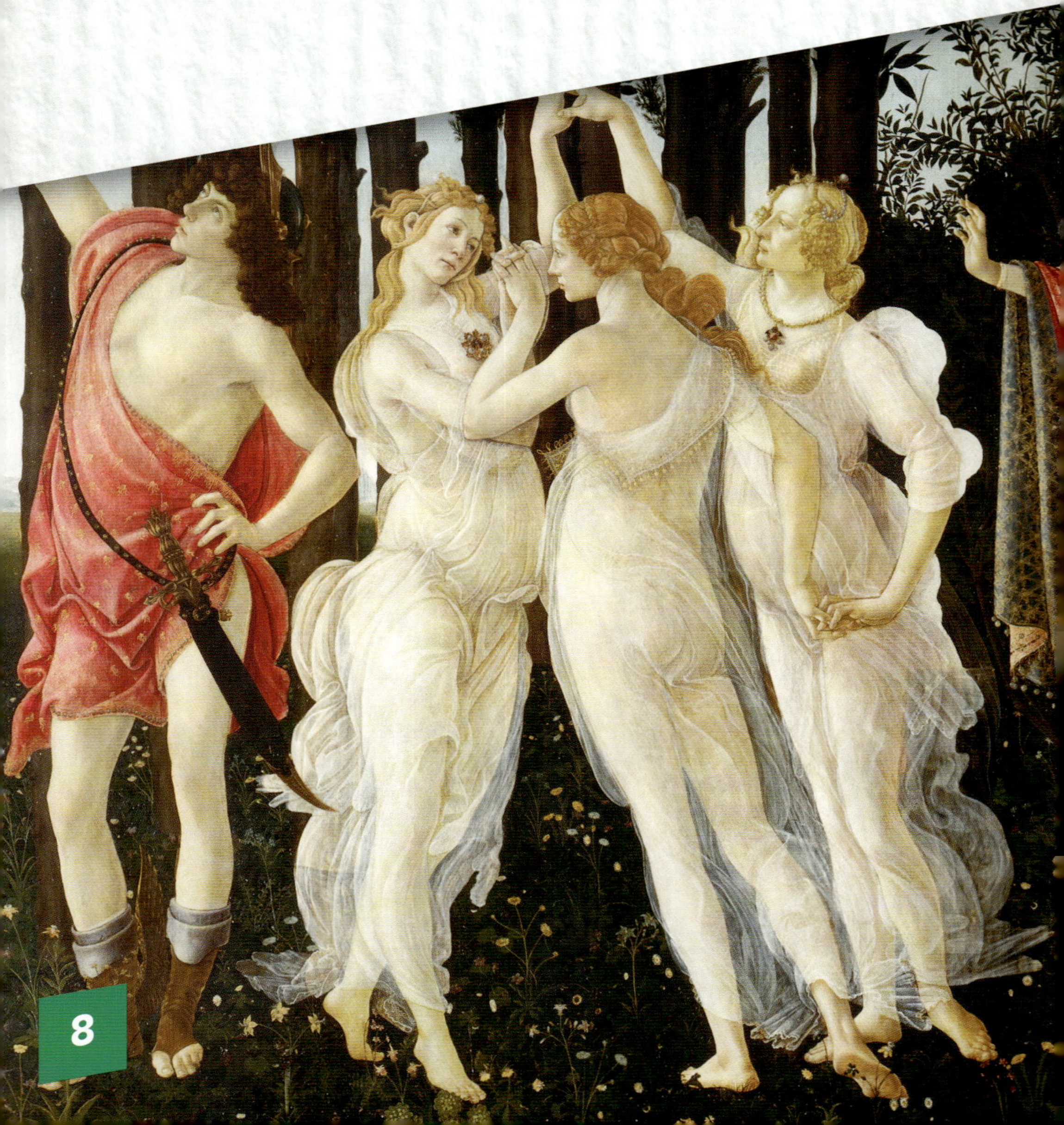

Artists could focus on their work without worrying about money.

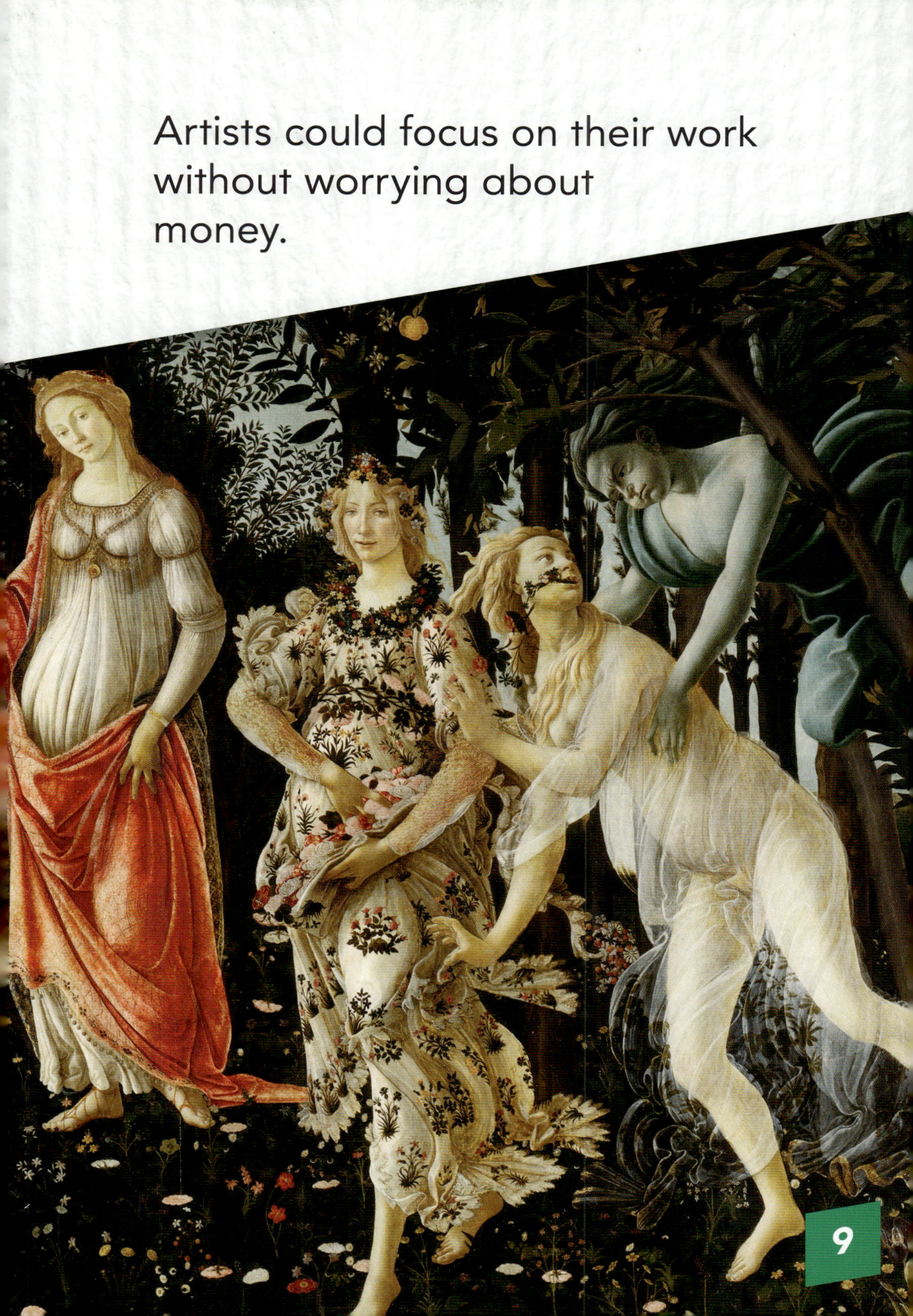

Renaissance Art

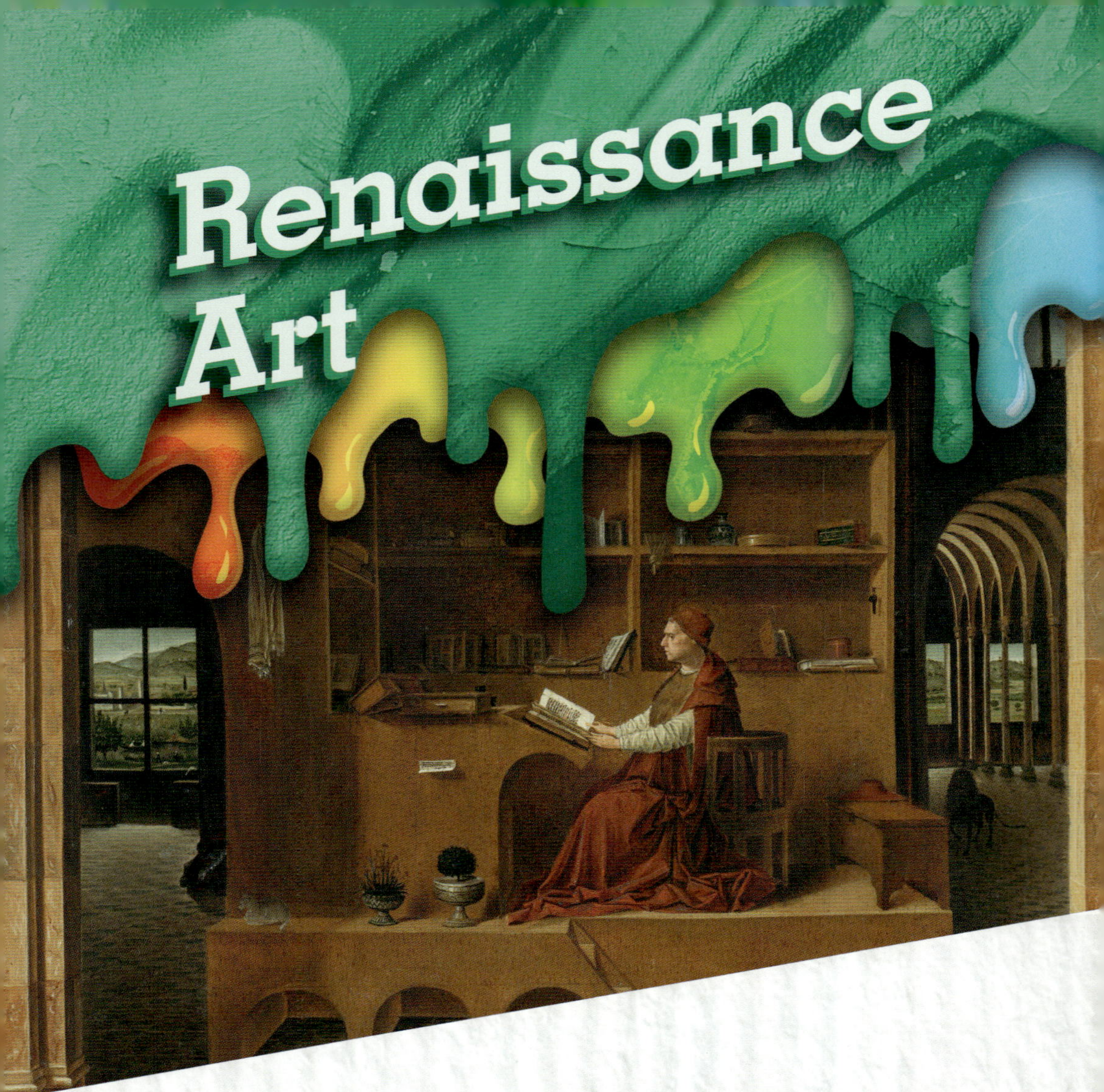

There were two main periods in the art movement. Artists of the Early Renaissance (1400–1479) tried to copy Classical Art. They focused on form and **symmetry**.

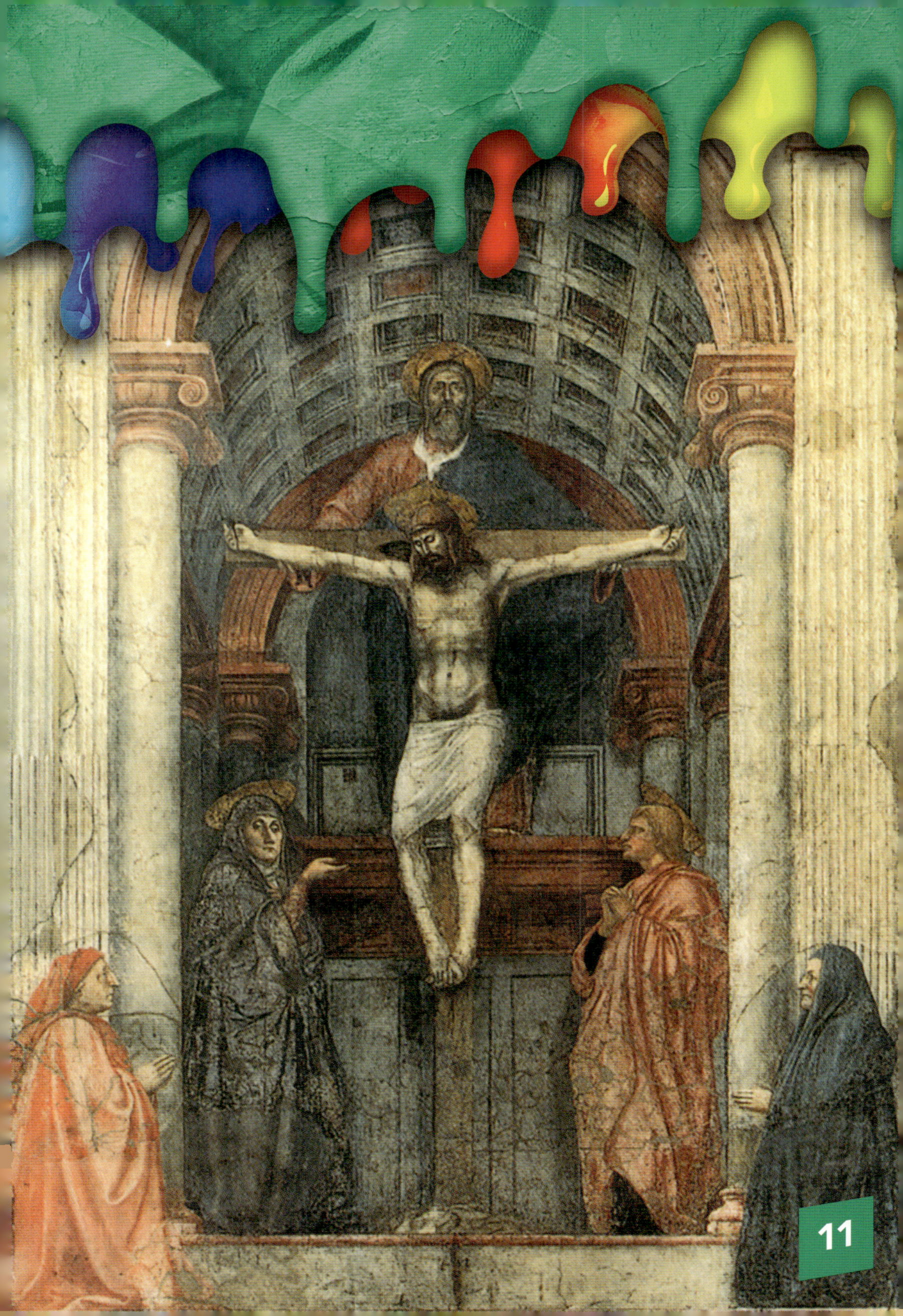

Artists of the High Renaissance (1475–1525) showed an interest in space and **perspective**. They concentrated on **realism**. Many artists of this time painted on ceilings and domes.

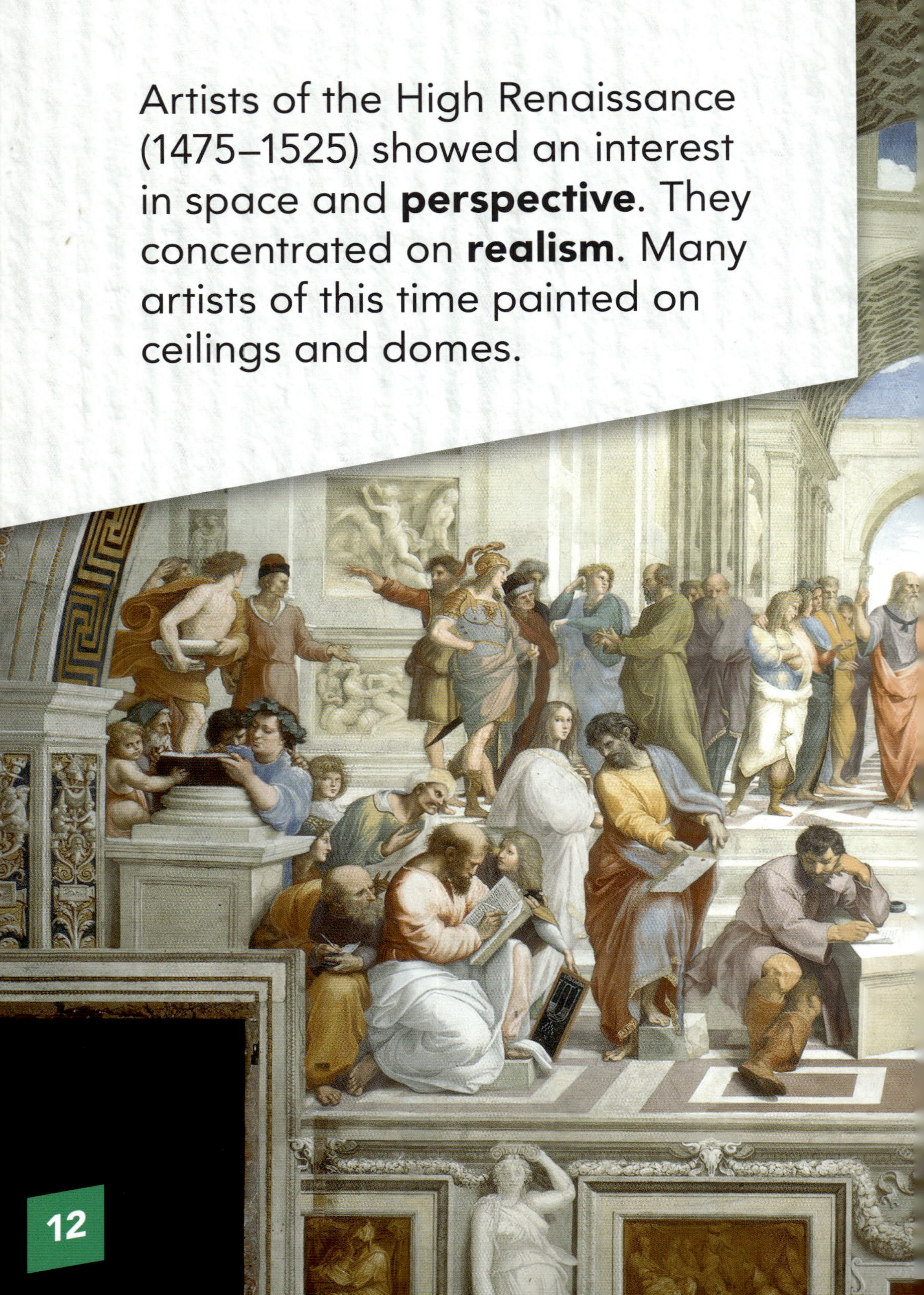

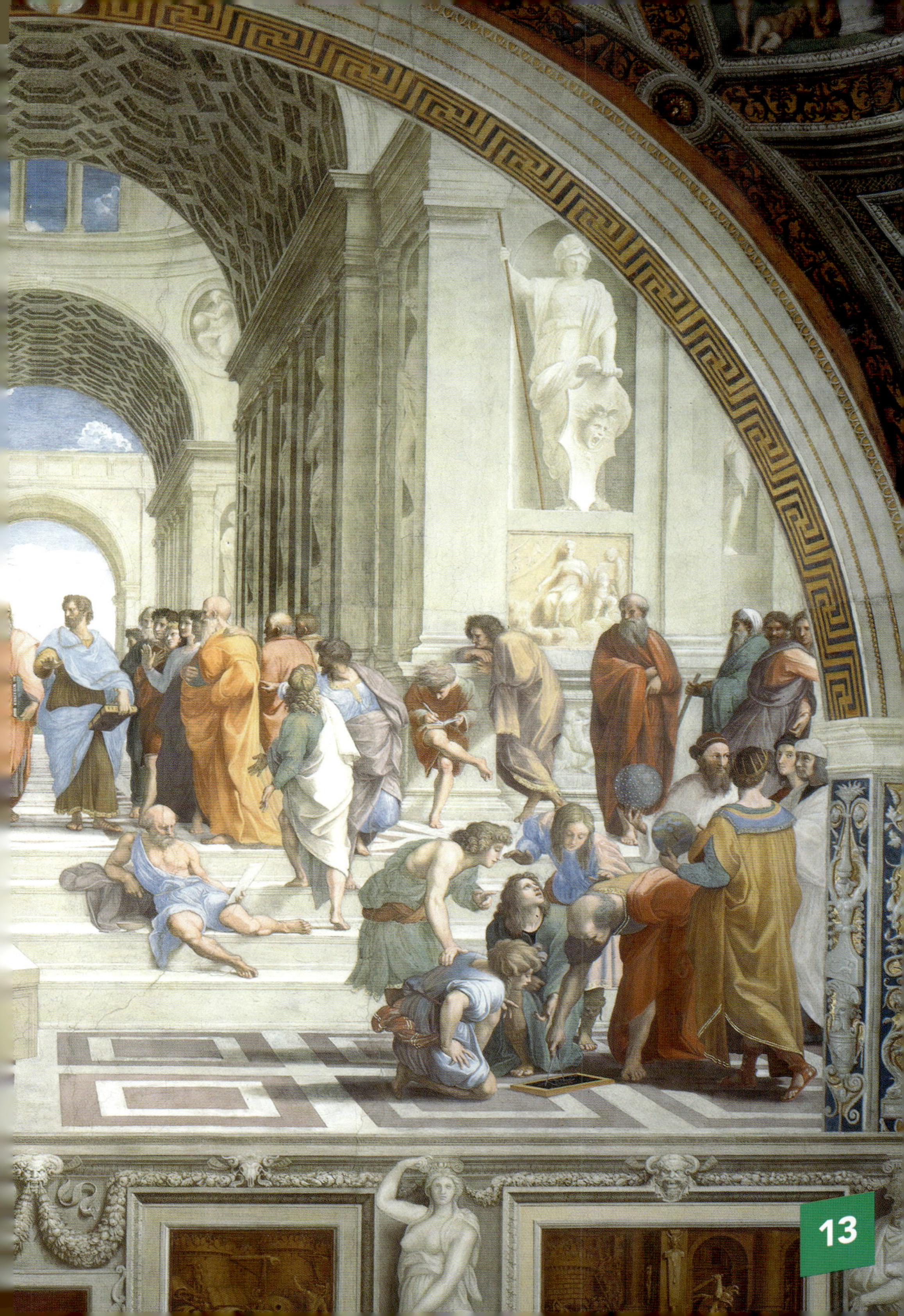

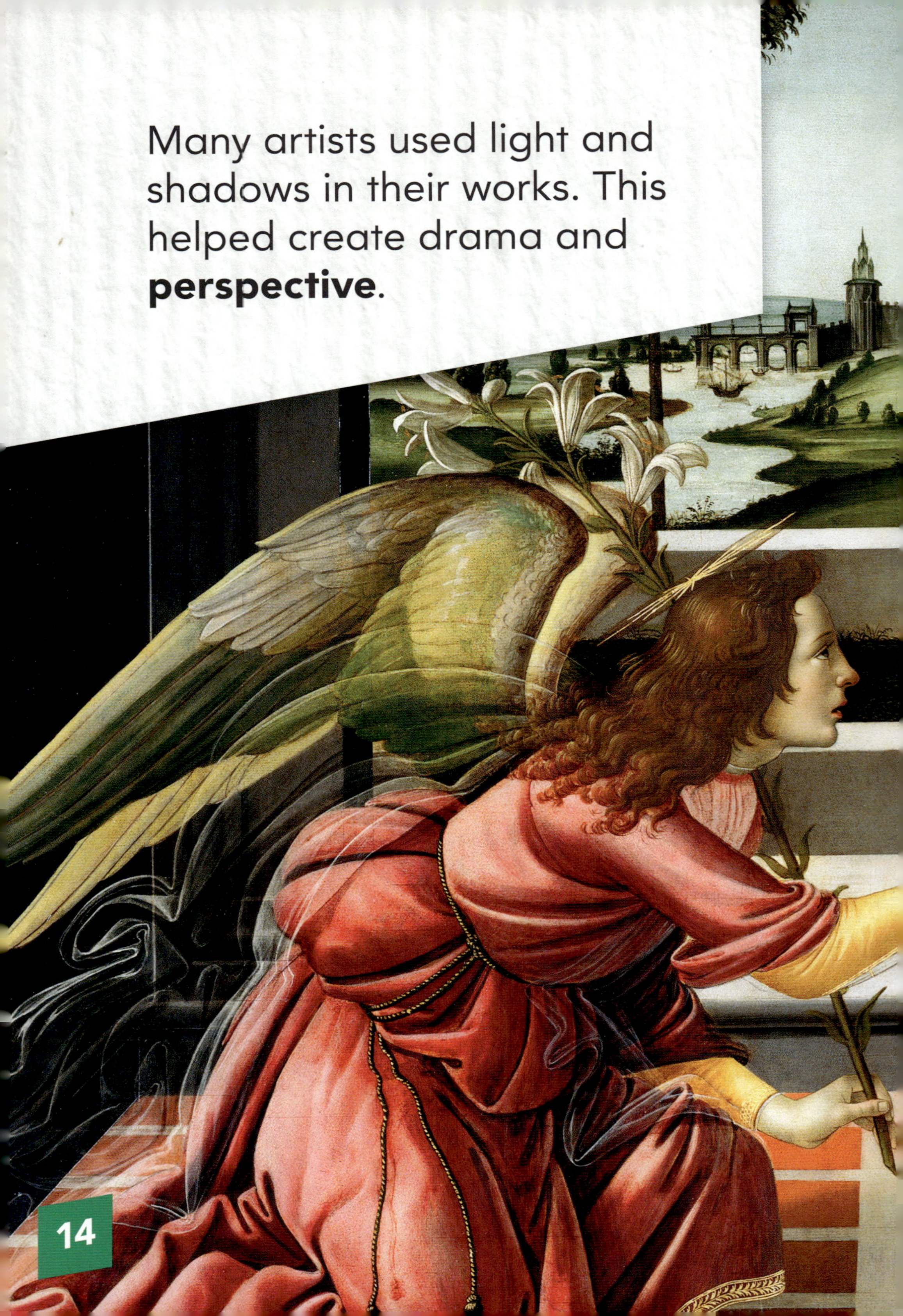

Many artists used light and shadows in their works. This helped create drama and **perspective**.

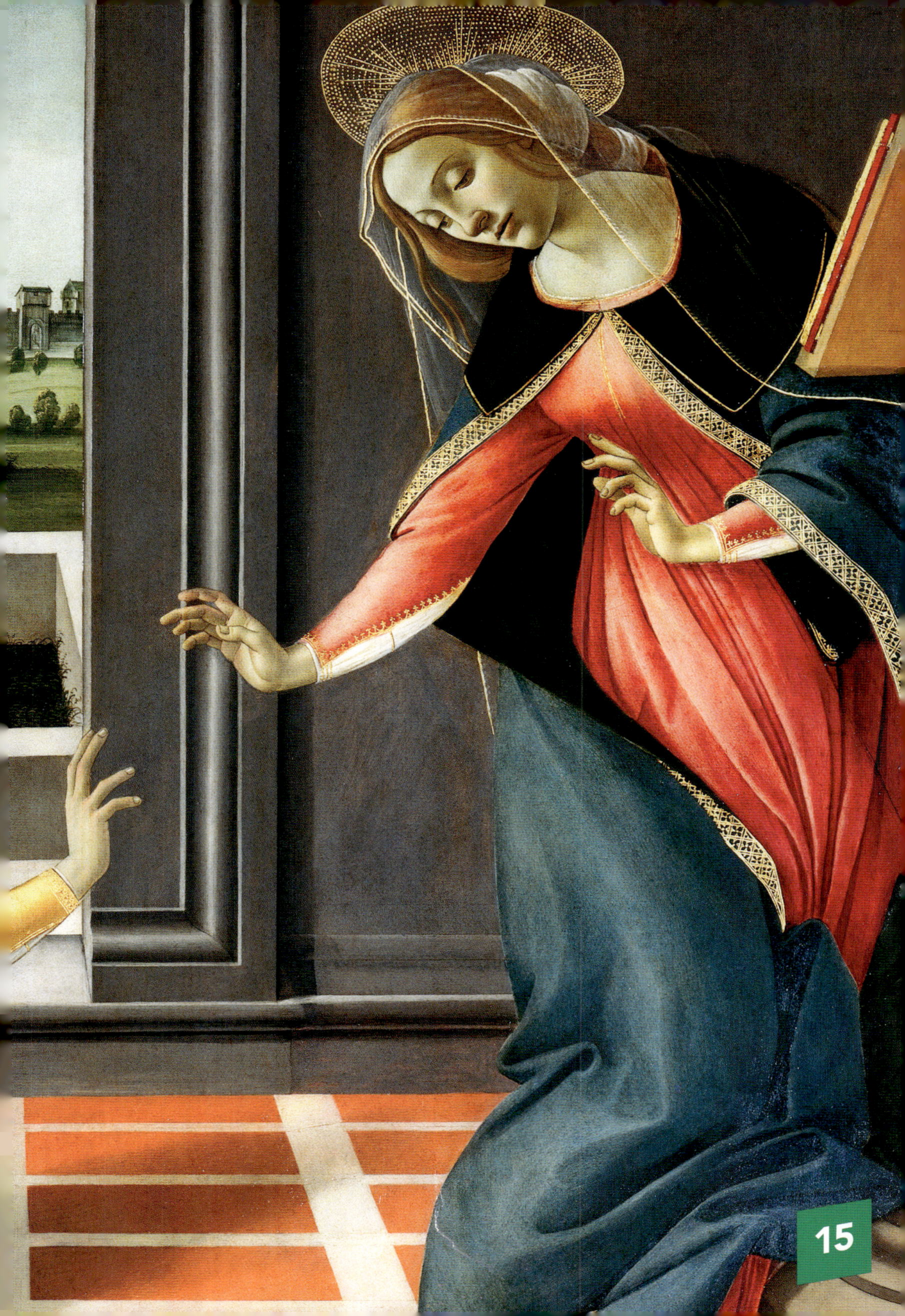

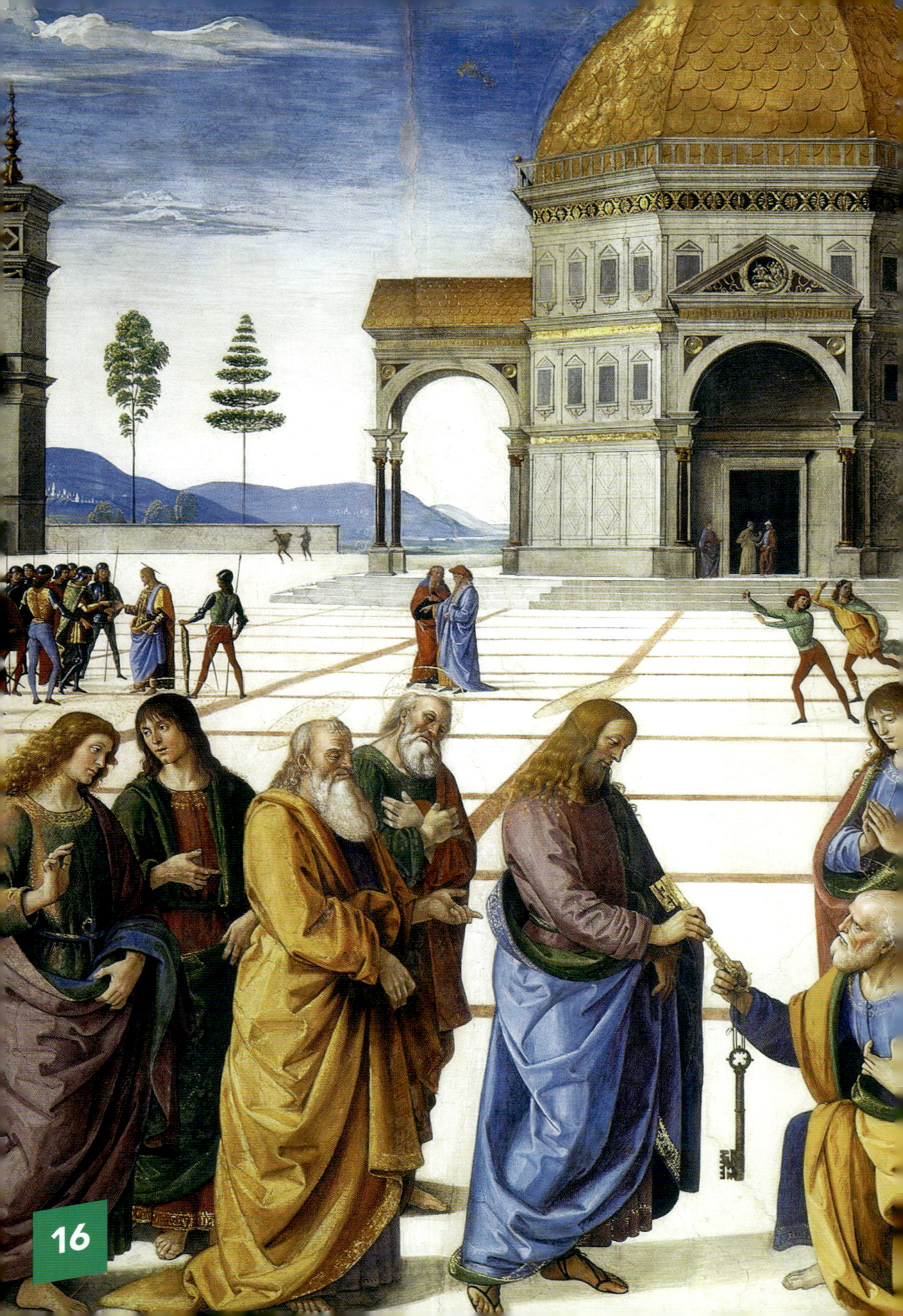

16

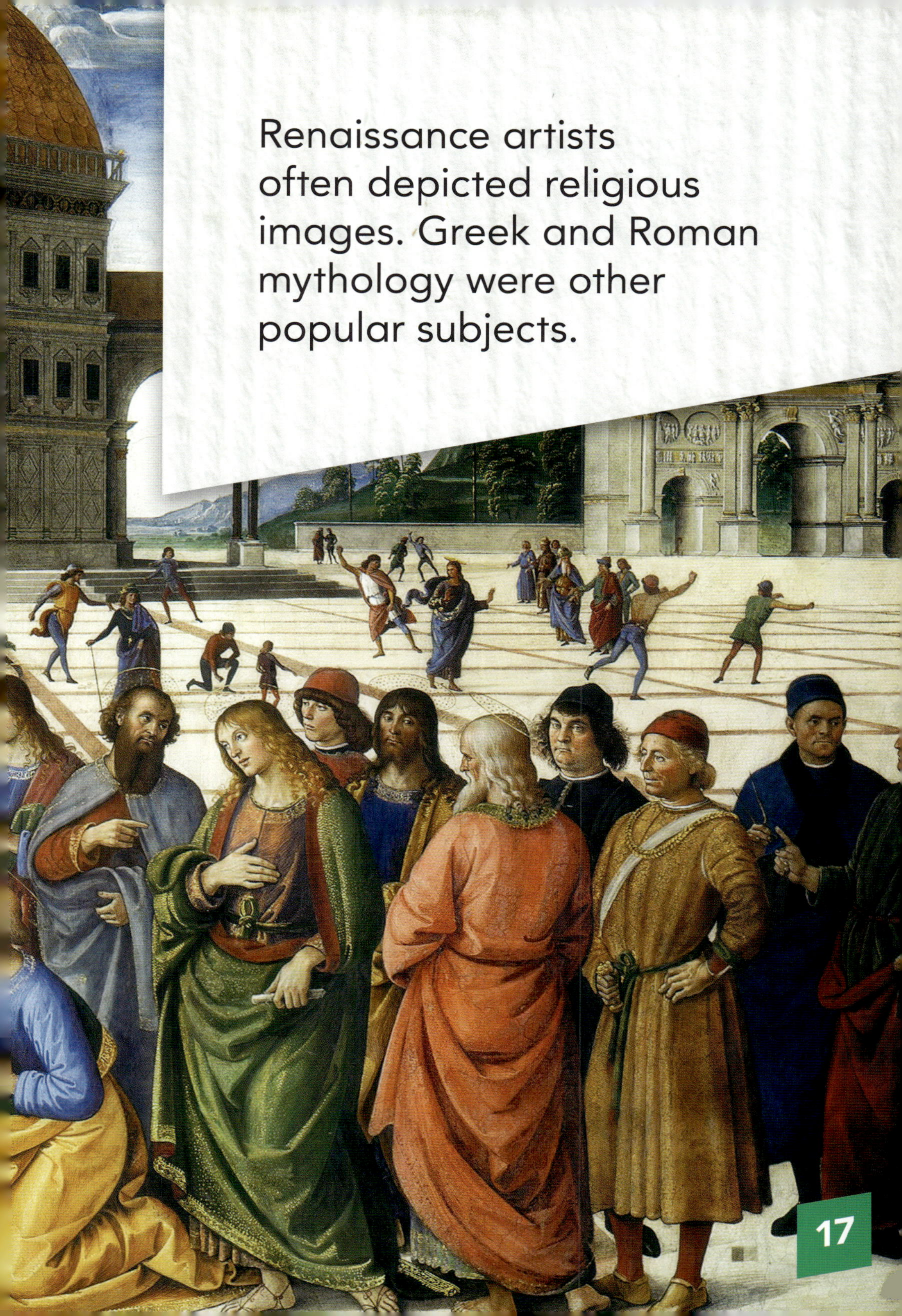

Renaissance artists often depicted religious images. Greek and Roman mythology were other popular subjects.

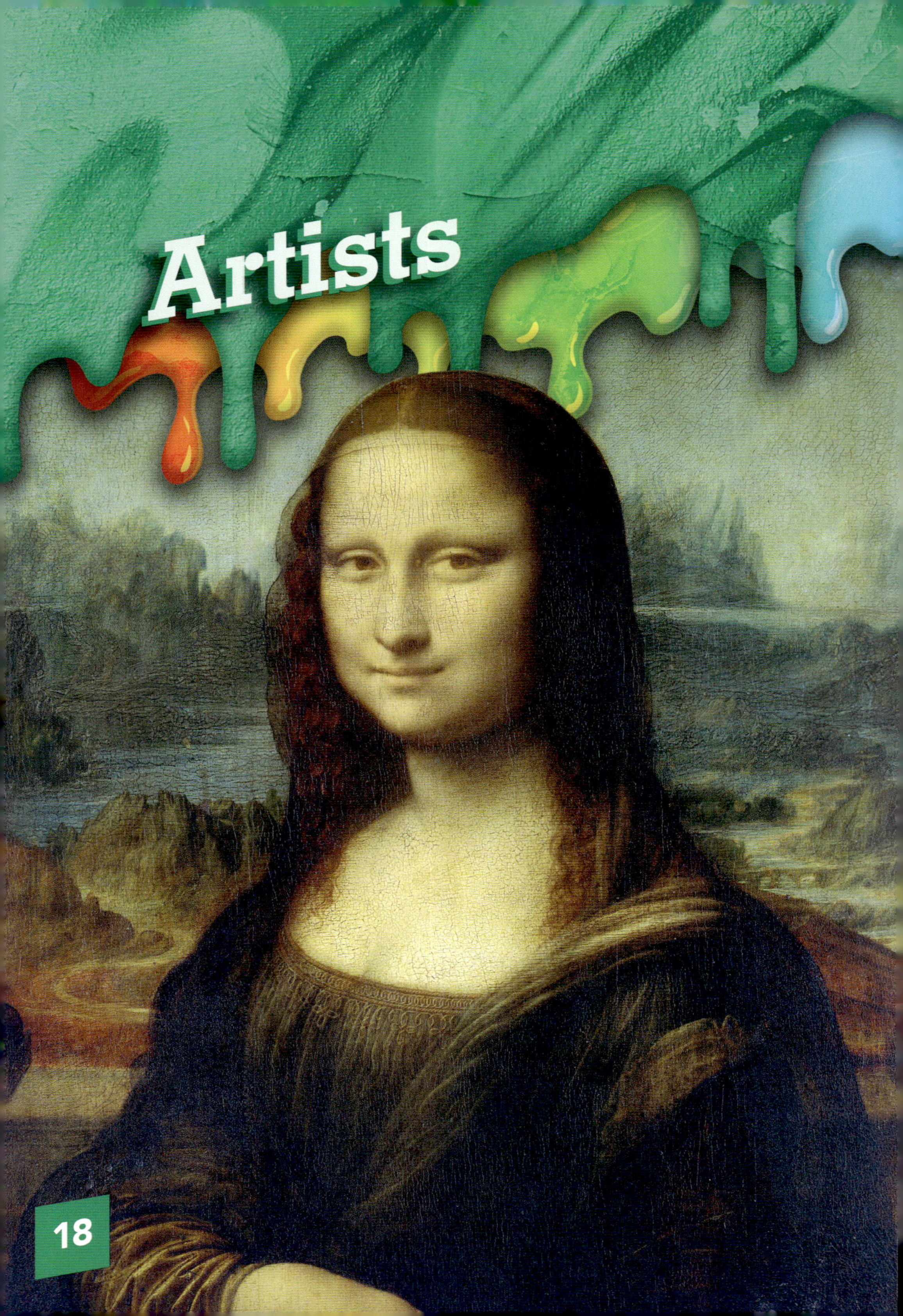

Artists

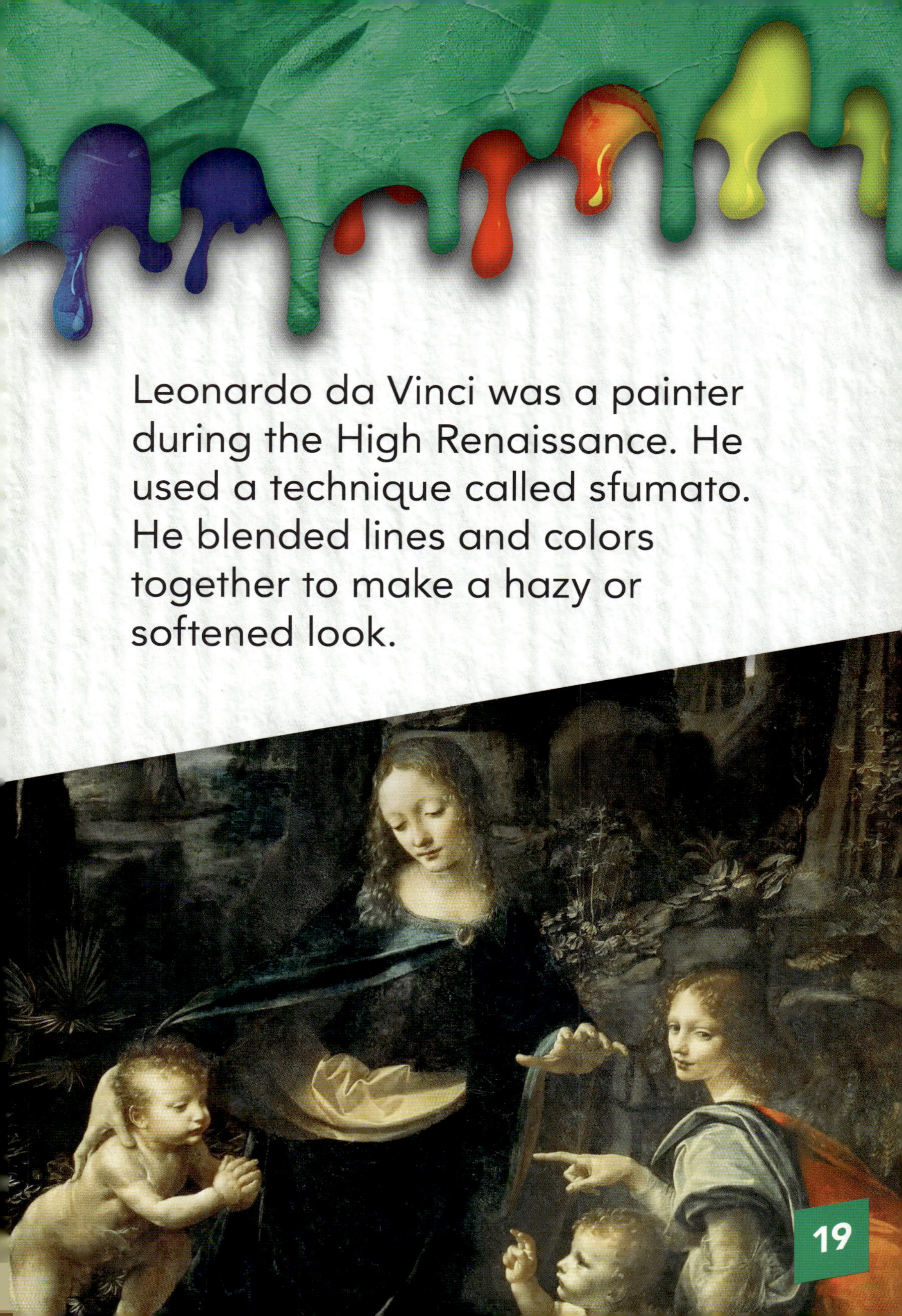

Leonardo da Vinci was a painter during the High Renaissance. He used a technique called sfumato. He blended lines and colors together to make a hazy or softened look.

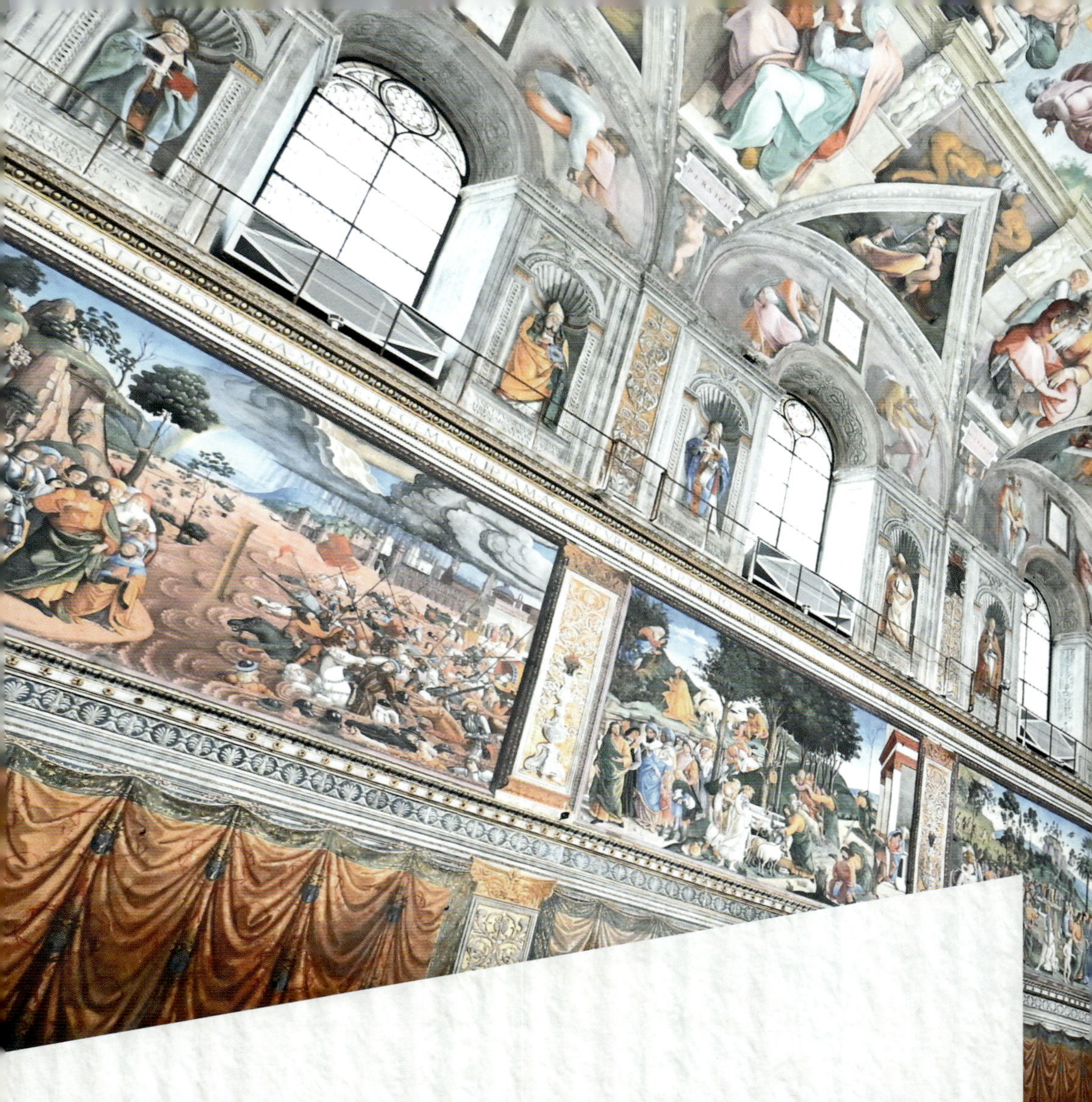

Michelangelo was a sculptor and a painter. Many of his sculptures were inspired by the human body. He spent more than four years painting the ceiling of the Sistine Chapel in Rome, Italy.

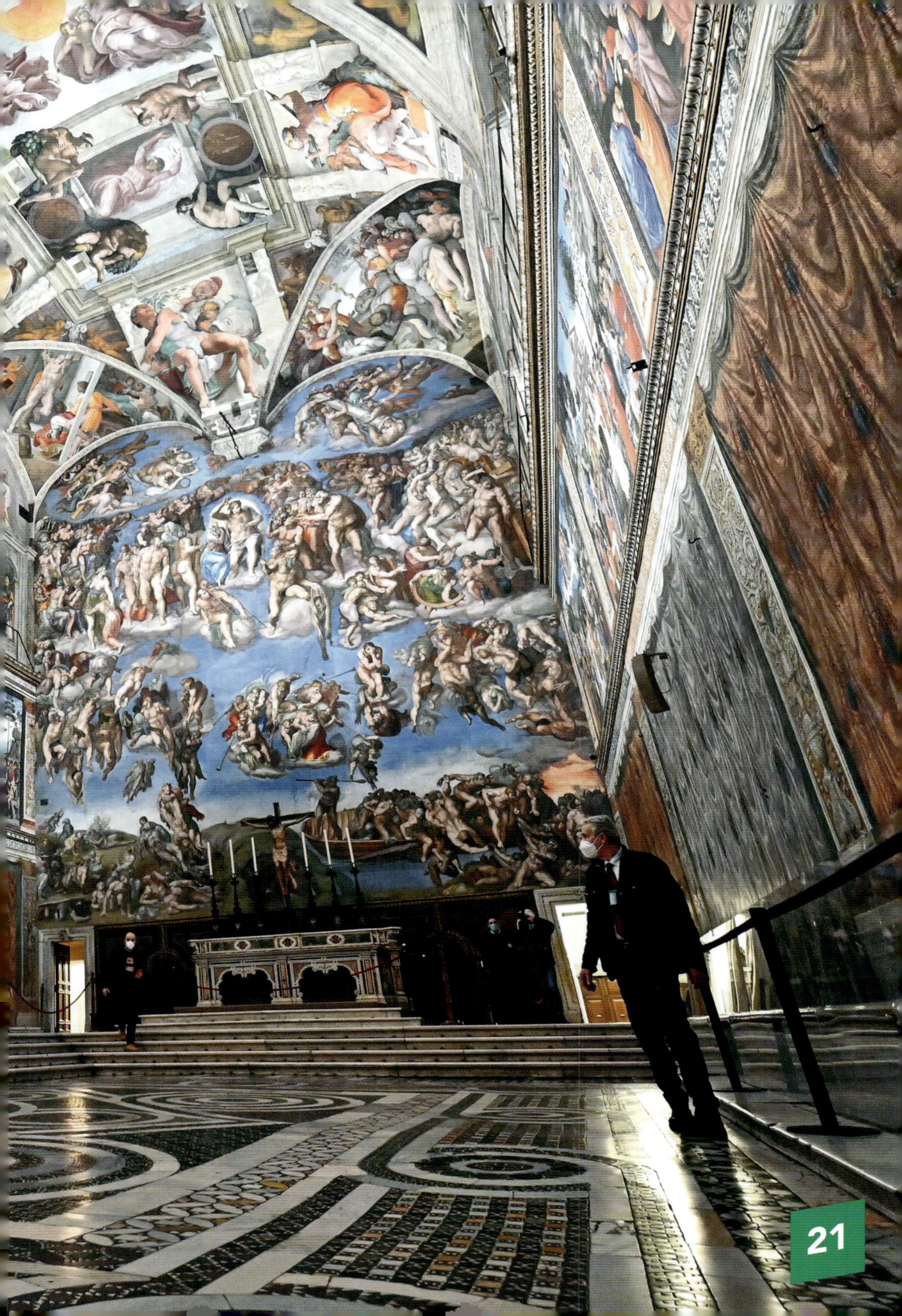

More Facts

- The word "Renaissance" comes from a French word meaning "rebirth."
- Leonardo da Vinci was skilled in many areas. He studied geology, botany, anatomy, and flight.
- Donatello was a famous artist from the Early Renaissance. He was a talented sculptor.

Glossary

humanism – a mode of thought that gives highest importance to human values and achievements. This was reflected in Renaissance art, especially with the study of the human body.

perspective – a way of showing objects on the flat surface of a picture so that they seem the correct size and distance from one another.

realism – a movement in the fine arts that is concerned with representing things as they actually are or as they are normally seen.

symmetry – a state in which both sides of something are balanced in size, form, or arrangement.

Index

Online Resources

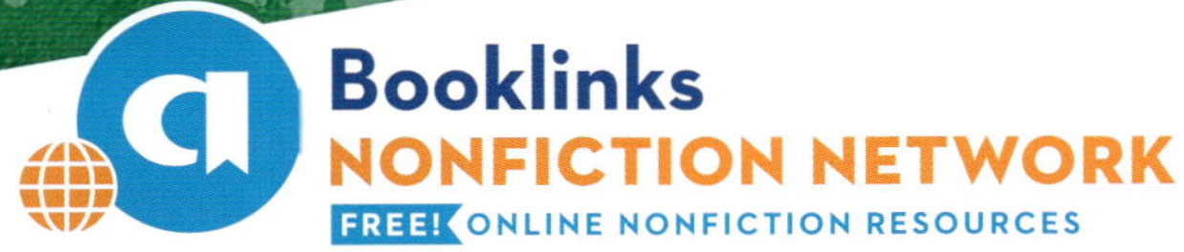

To learn more about Renaissance art, please visit **abdobooklinks.com** or scan this QR code. These links are routinely monitored and updated to provide the most current information available.